Pebble™ Plus

Under the Sea
Jellyfish

by Carol K. Lindeen

Consulting Editor: Gail Saunders-Smith, PhD
Consultant: Jody Rake, Member
Southwest Marine/Aquatic Educator's Association

Capstone
press

Mankato, Minnesota

Pebble Plus is published by Capstone Press
151 Good Counsel Drive, P.O. Box 669, Mankato, Minnesota 56002
www.capstonepress.com

1 2 3 4 5 6 09 08 07 06 05 04

Library of Congress Cataloging-in-Publication Data
Lindeen, Carol K., 1976–
   Jellyfish / by Carol K. Lindeen.
   p. cm.—(Pebble Plus: Under the sea)
   Includes bibliographical references (p. 23) and index.
   ISBN 0-7368-2600-9 (hardcover)
   1. Jellyfishes—Juvenile literature. [1. Jellyfishes.] I. Title. II. Series.
QL377.S4L49 2005
593.5'3—dc22   2003025610

Summary: Simple text and photographs present the lives of jellyfish.

Editorial Credits
Martha E. H. Rustad, editor; Juliette Peters, designer; Kelly Garvin, photo researcher;
   Karen Hieb, product planning editor

Photo Credits
Herb Segars/gotosnapshot.com, cover
Jeff Rotman, 18–19
Minden Pictures/Chris Newbert, 20–21
Paul Sutherland Photography/sutherlandstock.com, 14–15
PhotoDisc Inc., back cover; Sami Sarkis, 1
Seapics.com/Bob Cranston, 8–9; Espen Rekdal, 12–13; Jim Knowlton, 16–17; Richard Herrmann, 4–5;
   Scott Leslie, 6–7, 10–11

Note to Parents and Teachers

The Under the Sea series supports national science standards related to the diversity and unity of life. This book describes and illustrates jellyfish. The images support early readers in understanding the text. The repetition of words and phrases helps early readers learn new words. This book also introduces early readers to subject-specific vocabulary words, which are defined in the Glossary section. Early readers may need assistance to read some words and to use the Table of Contents, Glossary, Read More, Internet Sites, and Index/Word List sections of the book.

Word Count: 95
Early-Intervention Level: 14

Table of Contents

Jellyfish

What are jellyfish?

Jellyfish are invertebrates.

They have no bones.

Jellyfish are soft
like jelly. Their bodies
are shaped like bells.

Some jellyfish grow
bigger than a person.
Some jellyfish are
as small as a penny.

Stinging

Jellyfish have many tentacles.

Each tentacle can sting.

Jellyfish sting other animals
with their tentacles.
Prey cannot move
after being stung.

Jellyfish pull their prey
into their mouths.

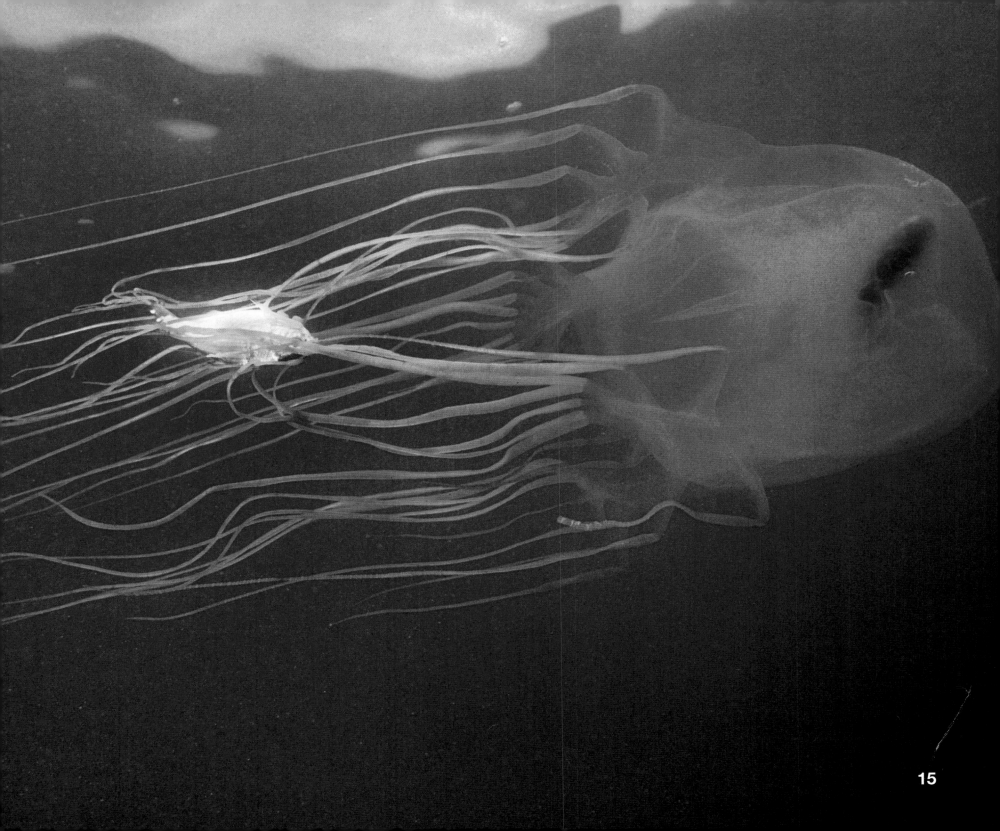

Some fish swim near jellyfish
to stay safe from predators.
The predators avoid jellyfish
and their stings.

Jellyfish sometimes gather

in groups called smacks.

Under the Sea

Jellyfish swim and float
under the sea.

Glossary

invertebrate—an animal without a backbone or any other bones

predator—an animal that hunts other animals for food; jellyfish predators include sea turtles, fish, and snails.

prey—an animal that is killed and eaten by another animal; jellyfish prey includes fish and shrimp.

smack—a group of jellyfish

sting—to hurt with a sharp, venomous tip; a jellyfish stings other animals with its tentacles.

tentacle—a thin, flexible arm on some animals; many tentacles hang from the body of a jellyfish.

Read More

Dornhoffer, Mary K. *Jellyfish*. First Reports. Minneapolis: Compass Point Books, 2004.

McKenzie, Michelle. *Jellyfish Inside Out.* Monterey, Calif.: Monterey Bay Aquarium, 2003.

Rustad, Martha E. H. *Jellyfish*. Ocean Life. Mankato, Minn.: Pebble Books, 2003.

Internet Sites

FactHound offers a safe, fun way to find Internet sites related to this book. All of the sites on FactHound have been researched by our staff.

Here's how:

1. Visit *www.facthound.com*

2. Type in this special code **0736826009** for age-appropriate sites. Or enter a search word related to this book for a more general search.

3. Click on the **Fetch It** button.

FactHound will fetch the best sites for you!

Index/Word List